At the Lake with Heisenberg

Poems by Robert L. Dean, Jr.

Kansas City   Spartan Press   Missouri

Spartan Press

Kansas City, Missouri

spartanpresskc@gmail.com

Copyright (c) Robert L. Dean, Jr., 2018
First Edition 1 3 5 7 9 10 8 6 4 2
ISBN: 978-1-946642-85-1
LCCN: 2018962482

Design, edits and layout: Jason Ryberg
Cover art: Jon Lee Grafton
Author photo: Cole Dean
All rights reserved. No part of this publication may be reproduced or transmitted in any form or by any means, electronic or mechanical, including photocopying, recording or by info retrieval system, without prior written permission from the author.

Spartan Press would like to thank Prospero's Books,
The Fellowship of N-finite Jest, The Prospero Institute
of Disquieted P/o/e/t/i/c/s, Will Leathem, Tom Wayne,
Jeanette Powers, j. d. tulloch, Jon Bidwell, Jason Preu,
Roy Beckemeyer, Mark McClane, Tony Hayden and the
whole Osage Arts Community.

The author gratefully acknowledges the editors and staff of
the following publications, in which versions of the following
poems first appeared, sometimes in different forms
or under different titles:

The Ekphrastic Review: "Nighthawks," "Llama, 1957."
Flint Hills Review: "Upon Waking She Finds This Note,"
"Spacemen," "Cleanup on Aisle Five."
Heartland! Poetry of Love, Resistance & Solidarity: "O Beautiful."
I-70 Review: "At the Lake with Heisenberg."
Illya's Honey: "Birds," "Able to Leap," "Aria for Abandoned Sock,"
"That Side of the World," "Yes the Killers," "Seconds."
Red River Review: "Walking Ms. Dog," "The Viewing," "River,"
"They Run Free like a River of Wild Horses," "Sallee's Sallon."
River City Poetry: "Return of the Carver," "Chair Car," "Up,"
"This Last Deep Blue Day."
The Wichita Broadside Project: "In the Dreamtime,"
"Piatt Street, 1965."
"Chair Car" also appeared in *The Ekphrastic Review.*
"Birds" also appeared in *The Wichita Broadside Project.*
"Yes the Killers" also appeared in *Heartland! Poetry of Love,
Resistance & Solidarity.*

A NOTE ABOUT THE ART
AND A WORD OF THANKS

Four of the poems in this book are ekphrastic, written to particular works of visual art. It is not feasible to include the art itself in the present book, for various reasons. Therefore, I have included, at the end of each of these four poems, a QR code that will take readers to a web page displaying the particular piece of art which goes with that poem. For those of you without a QR scanner app, the four works of art have been listed in the back of this book along with the URLs which will take you to the art.

I would like to thank a few of the writing groups that have shaped and continue to shape who I am as a writer. The Basement Bards keep me on track: Roy and Pat Beckemeyer, Skyler Lovelace, Diane Wahto, and Dave Cook. The Kansas Authors Club provides camaraderie and wonderful networking. I learned much from the Dallas Poets Community, the Greater Dallas Writers Association, and especially the Wednesday Weirdos (you know who you are: get out the Likeastones!). Thanks to Jason Ryberg for having the patience to put this book together.

-Robert L. Dean, Jr.

CONTENTS

Preface

Birds / 1

Return of the Carver / 2

In the Dreamtime / 4

Romeo, Romeo / 5

Chair Car / 7

At the Lake with Heisenberg / 12

Able to Leap / 13

Zen and the Art of Spirit Photography / 14

Seventeen cats on the front steps of 82 Maple Street / 15

Aria for Abandoned Sock / 19

Walking Ms. Dog / 20

The Viewing / 21

Nighthawks / 23

River / 26

Upon Waking She Finds This Note / 28

O Beautiful / 29

That Side of the World / 31

Piatt Street, 1965 / 34

Yes the Killers / 35

Up / 37

Spacemen / 39

Cleanup on Aisle Five / 42

They Run Free like a River of Wild Horses / 45

Llama, 1957 / 47

Sallee's Sallon / 48

Seconds / 50

This Last Deep Blue Day / 52

PREFACE

My father has communicated with me twice since his death in 1995; the first time through the speakers of my car radio, the second time from the face of a penny on the floor of the local Dillons grocery store. Both times the language he used was unexpected, wordless. My mother, who died in 1992, has chosen, for whatever reasons, to remain silent, though her touch is always upon me. You will find them both in the pages which follow, along with others who have come and gone in my life, both real and imaginary.

The brilliant slipstream novelist Patricia Anthony, one of the real, who makes an appearance here, closes her final book, *Flanders,* with an unfinished letter from the protagonist, Travis Lee Stanhope, written from his dugout on the battlefield to his younger brother back in Texas: *You listen careful now, Bobby, for I must tell you the most important secret: The black by the cypress looks threatening, but beyond waits a calm and sparkling place. And if I never bequeath you anything else, I give you this certainty: That shimmer I've seen is the power of the universe. It runs through me and you, through the dead men in the field and through the rats that eat them. It's love. Funny how simple*

And that is it, the end, breaking off in mid-sentence. In my childhood, my family called me Bobby, and I feel as if Patricia is speaking to me here, as indeed she often did when we got together for conversation and green tea at her townhome in Dallas. We spoke of many things. Language, of course, as writers will, but also the Little Grays of ufology, spiritualism, Zen, tarot, quantum mechanics, string theory. Patricia believed in all these things, while I played my designated part of sceptic. Heisenberg, Schrödinger, Born and others joined us frequently, channeling themselves though Patricia, while I channeled Einstein's objection *God does not play dice.* Once, during a discussion of charm and strangeness, or some such stuff, Patricia explained that the table between us was not really solid, not really *there.* My answer was a rapping of my knuckles on the wood, which produced a solid knocking sound, and the insistence I had not only proven her wrong but disproved the entire theory of quantum mechanics. Patricia laughed and chalked it up to Zen.

    Of all the people I've known, Patricia Anthony is the one person I would have expected to communicate with me after her death. But, alas, after her disincarnation in 2013, not a word. I take this as a good sign, that she achieved whatever it was she believed she was supposed to achieve. I also believe, as somewhat of a Taoist, that every time I breathe I inhale and exhale a little bit of Patricia Anthony, a bit of the *ch'i,* the life force that permeates everything, much as Travis Lee Stanhope describes in his interrupted final letter home.

    Communication. Language. As poets, we are supposed to know how it works. Rap on our tables, be they pen and paper or computer keyboards, and produce—what, exactly? Charm, perhaps? Strangeness? Read the passage from Patricia's novel again: *That shimmer I've seen is the power of the universe. It runs through me and you…it's love. Funny how simple*

    Fill in the blank. Or, better yet, don't.

*Where can I find a man who has forgotten words
so I can have a word with him?*

-*Chuang Tzu*, translated by Burton Watson

Birds

The word is barely out of her mouth
and the evening is full of the songs of them,
the air electric with the possibility of flight.

Cars, she says, and Dopplered breezes
of humanity blue shift-red shift on Douglas
Avenue, small bits of a universe with places to go.

Life, her palms upturned in praise of time and space,
and the tinnitus of years, the cacophony of what I've always
   thought of
as language, is suddenly gone, and I understand

that this is the way the world talks: not just two people
on a sidewalk conversing about conversing, but
the winking out of lights in a bookstore,

the texture of an orange sun sinking into a violet cloud,
the smell of the promise of rain,
the sound of night on its way, and the rending of it,

the taste of the eternal on the lips of a moment:
realize with the clarity of Lazarus rising
the difference between not moving and standing still.

Return of the Carver

I ghost this
graveyard of a day
ciphering names
worn to the bone
names yet to be chiseled
stone wombs pregnant with names

absence of shadow
shadows me
absence of footsteps
falling
prayers
flutter after me
folded hands reach out
lamentations
without mouths
lacerate flesh
in absentia

down this path
a whisper of lilac
lichened cherubs
wings clipped
fountains from which
no salvation flows

and here in the
still center
the eye
weeping I reach out touch
gnarled oak
scarred deaths
though the heart arrow-pierced
beats still
my ear drums shatter
bleed
names again
to be uttered
only when the sky speaks

In the Dreamtime

the Grandfathers rise. Bleached bones
bind with sinew, flesh, breathe back
sky, earth, four winds, smoke

the pipe of always return, as long as
grass grows, water flows. Stomp-stomp thunder
dance, bellow-snort songs of rut. The stars,

they say: all that and more.
Run with us.

Romeo, Romeo

Another town, departure, lover thrown under the bus. The baggage compartment's full and you can't afford an extra seat and you've packed light as usual. This stop's a dump like all the rest, and you should know. The bus can't pull out quick enough for you. You'd enjoy the scenery, strike up a conversation, but you've seen it all before and you're the only passenger and it's the dead of night. But that's the way you wanted it. You called ahead just to make sure. Got the through bus, no stops. Through to where, you don't know. But you're aboard and you're going. When you get there, nobody will meet you, but that's just who you're traveling to see. Space is what you need right now, and lots of it. In the mirror, the driver's face is blank, like yours this morning when you shaved, as if he too knows that moving on's a bitch.

Chair Car
From the painting by Edward Hopper, American, 1965.

Not important is where they are going
is where they are coming from
here is where they are now is
this train moving is
this a train is

not as important as the light
how it

infuses everything
with the clarity of cataracts
illuminates nothing outside the windows

is the sky the vaulted interior of this car of seats half empty is
the interior the sky half full of light on a gray day refracted
into the interiors into wherever whoever they are now
these four passengers

retracting
destinations departures any sense of journey

or could this be it

manicured rows of hedged chairs
blunt tongued fescue door mats stuck out

licking
light like meat cleavers down the center aisle
licking
light like square-booted one-legged giant
tracks some limb-lopped ticket puncher
coming or going left
some monk of the crippled always here to always there
    always
neither here nor there passing shroud wrapped in light
through this cloister of passing
unnoticed unimportance
punching no tickets punch left in
the next or before car anyway
if there is one anyway
they don't have tickets anyway don't need
a pass for this any way you can tell from
their faces what you can see of them
anyway whatever
these scattershot passengers are or are not
passing to or from

and this is important

the door
the door at the far end
what the door at the far end of this car
doesn't have
a handle

is what we can't quite get
on this picture
out of this scenario
is what we can't quite get

how the light bathes
so completely the blonde woman so
shall we say it
radiantly yet
unenlighteningly her

right ankle hosiery the same opaque sheen as the scenery
behind her not passing by her face down-drawn
drawing us to it the light like a prayer
in her hands unopened a book
given or received in passing an offering to
or from the light-footed usher who has just
passed has yet to pass is always passing
just out of frame behind the door maybe hiding invisible
    impossible
to open but ajar slightly

and this is important

not open is her face
like light through a window seen
from a street but not the lamp
purse slipping forgotten pocket of days

this day that day always the same dark verdurous day
slipping from between her slightly blushed knee and the
    proximate arm of the chair
is this what the

black-haired bound-haired woman one seat up and across
seat odd-angled watches
the light
not illuminating past her tight-lipped mouth
her sharp nose
angling her closed book gaze at the
closed book or
verdant time slipping away
or is she
that one darkened key-hole eye she allows us to see
    anyway
the illuminato
the hidden clue
the sharp point of a midnight pump emerging
like a jab at the causeway of
day after day after day
pointing zig zag
to the next woman up
a bit of face flash of neck seep of brown hair
blue-hatted or green-hatted maybe
a shadow of doubt maybe over her ultramarine
shoulder maybe just barely light-touched a bit of
hand tiny bit we can't tell maybe
knitting maybe folded with some
unseen other

and this is important oh surely this is important

where she's looking
the blue woman

across the aisle again
zig zag

stare at a head
just the back of a head
above an antimacassar gray day blue
like the light like the wall the cloister
door at the center of it
the end of it all the focus of this
slightly off-center perspective this
study in expansive claustrophobia
at which he stares like one does
on a blue gray day in the front hedge chair
the only man in this car of hedged bet chairs
somewhat abstractedly pondering

zig zag zig zag zig

the spot where there has never been
never will be
anything to grab onto
wondering
perhaps like us

if this is important if
this is still life

Chair Car, Edward Hopper, 1965

At the Lake with Heisenberg

One duck,
a white buoy

riding the ripples
of winter blowing in,

head disappearing
like a particle in flux

into the nether regions,
tail raised towards an uncertain sky,

a little flag of defiance
in this roll-of-the-dice world,

an anchor dropped upwards
for the seeing from the unseen.

And if just one of us turns away, one only
cold-shoulders this chance vignette,

what then, Werner? What then?

Able to Leap

For Les

I loosen my tie, only to find you've gone.
Oh I know it's been years; but hey, I just figured

you'd always have my back.　　　　　It's not my fault
they don't make those phone booths anymore.

> The ones we leapt out of
> in the cottonwood-drifting sunlight,
> safety-pinned bath towels fluttering
> from our tee shirts.

Metropolis crumbles.　　　　　And me
with these silly fake glasses.

Zen and the Art of Spirit Photography
For Patricia Anthony

pumping the hand of the man with the camera when
    embers ignite
at the backs of my eyes and I say, still tipsy from blitzkrieg
    homage

    Sorry, I think there's someone

unthreading the banquette chair needle
back-pedaling space and time
sloshing hellos in laps of strangers, till

fragile
wet-winged
infant-eyed

small wonder, I passed right by

    I can't believe it's
    Yes, isn't it

enfolding, finally, each into other
the click of the Nikon sun

    Chrysalis, she said to me once, one sultry summer evening.

Seventeen cats on the front steps of 82 Maple Street
From the illustration by Edward Gorey,
American, 20th Century.

Yes, this is
the Cat Lady's house.
You remember

the Cat Lady. She lived
just down the street
or perhaps next door

or around the corner,
just as she does now, after
all these years, moves,

children, grandchildren,
wars and rumors of wars.
The very same

blue door
you knocked on,
after wading through

all those cats, rubbing up
against your legs and purring,
to collect for the paper route,

Halloween trick or treat—nothing
to be scared of, just a plump old lady in
tea-stained terry robe, pink curlers

and fuzzy slippers, and you could
count on her for at least a half dozen
Mars bars—and as time went on

all the lawn mowing, leaf raking,
gutter cleaning, TV antenna adjusting
you could handle, emergency runs

to the Save-A-Lot for milk and tuna,
and that time you repainted those steps
to better match the door only to find

dainty little pussy paw prints
all over your artwork the next day,
and here you are again, now, on this day,

older and wiser, you and your
granddaughter, knocking on that
blue door just down the street, around

the corner, next door, occupying
the same sunlit lot in your life
it will always have, the cats

rubbing up against Jenny's ankles
and purring, Jenny with
a half-dozen boxes of

Girl Scout cookies—Peanut Butter
Patties, of course—the sale
a foregone conclusion, and you wonder

what is on the other side of that
ancient, gracelessly ageing door,
if anyone has ever been invited

in—you haven't—whether the
smiles and snores of seventeen
plump cats can compensate

for whatever shadows skulk
inside. After the transaction, you spy
one autumn yellow maple leaf

at the foot of the steps
your grandson's rake missed
this morning, and, without knowing

why, you pick it up,
try to tuck it, carefully,
into your jacket pocket,

only to feel it crumble
into dust and slip
through your fingers,

just as it did
in childhood.

*Seventeen Cats on the front steps of 82 Maple Street,
Edward Gorey, 20th Century*

Aria for Abandoned Sock

A wave of the hand
and I am banished
to the dungeon
of lint and lost buttons
between dryer and wall.
It's true of course I'm no longer
that dashing young Argyle
in shiny wrapper
who caught your fancy
all those strides ago
beneath the Fashionable Footwear sign.
But how could you
sweep so tactlessly away
the dance of the fire on chill winter nights,
Dark Victory Bette Davis tears,
fudge ripple ice cream straight from the carton,
the trees in crimson and gold that day we buried
    Dulcinea,
the way I worshiped the ground you walked on,
the foot with which you walked upon it—
unless this cold-shouldered farewell
reflects the wry glint in your eye at which I wondered
when first you brought us home,
stripped us naked,
and slipped into my twin before me.

Walking Ms. Dog

*Ms. Dog stands on the shore
and the sea keeps rocking in
and she wants to talk to God.*

—Anne Sexton, *Hurry Up Please It's Time*

dark and stormy night but Ms. Dog must go out my
living room cypresses sway Ms. Dog keeps me on a short
leash her bleached bones clatter in the cold wind I ask
her why the carbon-monoxide-locked-garage-door thing
ah Bobby she says using my puppyhood name that's the
easy part the tough part Mommy's fur coat I'd never be
caught dead wearing pause sofa I hike a leg in the end
I say you just couldn't let go life still meant something
Ms. Dog jerks the leash I was a failed abortion Bobby in
the night in the kitchen above the butcher block counter
top Vinnie One Ear making swirling motions always
knew Ms. Dog says that candle-hat thing was baloney
don't you piss on the canvases Bobby I nearly choke she
yanks so hard only the dishwasher I whimper she studies
Vinnie's bloodless face you've almost got it she says pulls
a gun a little shot of this'll do it stars burst from Vinnie's
belly light years back to my office God I say I want to
die like that Ms. Dog flips her femur onto my desk well
then Bobby she aims the gun cocks the hammer up on
your hind paws slit your wrists let the ink flow I pluck
a galaxy from the sky flesh implodes the universe big-
bangs I crack the bone how sweet the marrow

The Viewing

Lifelike.
What you always wanted to be.

Formaldehyde
so much more permanent

than blood.
No more

heart murmurs
to keep you awake nights

wondering
what we will make of it when you're gone.

That phial of white beach stuff on the mantelpiece.
On what island

did you open yourself up
so much that it hurt.

Under which moon
did you pluck those ten thousand

god-grains from
naked flesh,

casket that one fleeting moment of
perfect penetration.

Don't worry dear.
Your secret is safe with us.

How natural you look this evening.

Nighthawks

From the painting by Edward Hopper, American, 1942.

Some broad's just tossed you
and you're strolling past this corner
joint with the wrap-around window and it's 3 AM
and the ceiling all lit up like a galaxy
with that new-fangled fluorescent crap
and you stop to watch the lonely planets
frozen inside, just you and the vacant-eyed
storefront peeping in from
across the street, you're
kinda curious to see what's gonna
happen, what kind of rumble's gonna
bust loose, three guys and one redhead
is always trouble, especially
with her dark cavern eyes
contemplating the sandwich she
holds up with one hand instead
of the snap-brimmed fedora sharpie
sitting next to her, hasta be the guy
she came in with, the guy whose hand
her free hand is not quite touching,
the guy staring sullenly ahead, cigarette
dripping from his fingers as if
something's finally sinking in
behind that hawk beak of a face
and it ain't what he walked in

expecting, and maybe the counterman's gonna
flourish an answer out from beneath
the countertop, he's certainly reaching
for something in his crisp white
uniform and soda jerk cap and it sure as hell
ain't coffee, three cups sitting neglected
at three cocked elbows, these guys,
these all-night countermen, they've
seen it all, heard it all, they're real
magicians, these guys, his lips are open
a crack, he's about to spill it, who she
will leave with, will it be
the bird that brung her, or maybe
that loner who's somehow managed
to find a shadow to lurk in on a stool
at the acute but somehow obtuse
angle of this triangle of an otherwise
reflective countertop, and he looks
familiar, this occluded moon
of human night, at least the bit of his mug
you can see anyway, you know this guy, you can
feel him, he's you, pondering the world
as it slips through your fingers, or would be, if
you walked in through that yellow door
at the back, and you know in a flash
the counterman's guess is wrong,
the trick is flubbed,
someone's switched out the rabbit,

cause that's just the door to the
kitchen, there is no ingress/egress
to this universe, even the counterman's
trapped in an orbit of polished Cherrywood,
and you realize how close the color is
to the woman's dress, hair, irradiated
brick across the street, as if she
planned all this when she gussied
herself up for this *tableau vivant,* this
final curtain call, realize with new-
fangled fluorescent clarity
Red's not leaving with Mr. Mystery,
she's tossing everything and everybody,
in a minute she'll toss that sandwich
and you and the storefront'll be keeping
those otherworldly coffee tureens on the back
counter company till the sun comes up,
you might as well light up a Phillies
like the sign above the window says
cause you ain't going nowhere neither.

Nighthawks, Edward Hopper, 1942

River

damned
toilet backed up
drowned clouds
float seaward across
linoleum sky
say this reminds me
baby whitecaps
whispering upstream
birthing secrets
downstream rippling
through here
someplace
the heartland, yes
remember
cool green blades under naked backs, we thought we saw
ships
castles
God, lying
about, ignoring
the sharpness of the world upon flesh
imagining anything
but this
ghastly, bloated
fish-nibbled
skin-sloughing

cipher
vomited up the porcelain
spillway of
somebody call
is somebody calling
plumber
dynamite
can anybody hear
echo, no
my heart
my damned heart
used to be a
river
flowing

Upon Waking She Finds This Note

When I am gone
burn me

When I am ash
                  scatter me

When I am wind
rippling tall grasses
               breathe me in

When I am river
     rushing toward ocean
 plumb me with one naked toe
but do not dam me

                           And when the
                  snow falls
and the night is at its longest
              and the moon is black
                      and the pillow has forgotten
                                only then

                      dream me

O Beautiful

Aleppo

A man begs us not to step over his family. He wears rags and tears and dust. Behind him a pile of rubble. Perhaps he once lived here. Perhaps also the legs and arms and heads before which he kneels. We do not know. We pass on by.

M10 hospital. We bandage. Stitch. Amputate. Slip, slide on blood, bowels. Don garments of stinking flesh. In a corner, a woman babbles, boy on a litter, eyes gone deaf. Windows shatter. Concrete dances. Barrel bomb. We burrow deeper. Carry wounded. Wounds. Dying. Death. What we carry, we become.

Ahead of us, a torch. Someone whispers: Crawl faster.

Sambisa Forest

When the men speak, it is not Chibok. Maybe Hausa. Arabic. They rip off the abaya, the niqab, the black they make us wear to cover our shame when it suits them, our only concealment, our one refuge, the cold ash of our village, our hearts. They ram into us, thighs banging buttocks. We are 14, 12, 8. Our mounds weep red. Husband, they say, in our language. Before the next one sticks it in.

Helicopters in the monkey-bread trees. Alone in our huts like graves. Blessed Virgin, we whisper: Blessed G.I. Joe. Machine guns. Rockets. Kaboom. Fingers laced, we listen. The hiss of snakes. The swagger of the husbands. What we are left with.

We eat bloody dates. Drink strange-leaved tea. Pledge mubaya'a. Birth their babies. Detonate in crowds of strangers. The husbands say we go to Paradise. And we do.

Juárez

The Dead Women haunt the maquiladoras. Assemble into printers, TVs, cars. Sigh spreadsheets in Wenatchee, dust up Sioux City back roads, number *Days of Our Lives* in Brooklyn. They tire of trash dumps, sewers, creosote, cactus. Gardens of red crosses.

Mummies grin on morgue slabs. Sons. Uncles. Brothers. Those we ransom two times, three. Fifteen-year-olds in Escalades and Yankees caps collect. Quinceañera bouquets wither. Carnicerías, discotecas fire the night.

Make-shift altars: tequila, Marlboros, the things She craves. Black candles. Mariachis sing: *Santa Muerte, Bony Lady, Lady of the Shadows, Lady of the Holy Death.* We shoulder grappling hooks, machetes. Wade the river. Shimmer in the moon's image. Tired. Poor. Huddled. What we are not: wretched.

Stars whisper. We climb. The eyes of gringo guns.

That Side of the World

As if it had an edge to it

As if, like a coin, she could flip it

As if it were paper
a crane, a butterfly, if only she knew the art of folding

As if wings
many, oh so many, fluttering upwards

As if thousands of breaths
breathed back into the clean blue face of the morning

As if people never plummeted past office windows
clothes billowing out like failed parachutes

As if eleven and nine were numbers in a game played
    only by children
ready or not

As if the game could never be replayed
is not now being replayed

crowds cheering
flags waving

...eight...
...seven...

As if half a continent were far enough
As if a decade

As if eight million souls couldn't hide her
As if fields of wheat could

As if, here, now, in this middle-of-nowhere hospital
she can

fluff a pillow
feel a pulse
make a mark on a chart
save someone

...six...
...five...

As if commandos dropping out of the night sky
As if terrorists descending

As if she could turn off all TVs
As if this side of the world

...four...
...three...

As if she could ever hate that much
As if the tissue she twists in her hands

As if there is any place left

…two…
…one…

As if the reporter's question
how she feels, today

…heads…
…tails…

As if bodies, inevitably

fall

The day after a team of U.S. Navy SEALs killed Osama Bin Laden, a local television reporter asked a nurse in Newton, Kansas, how she felt. Ten years earlier the woman had been at a desk on the fifth floor of the North Tower when the first plane struck. The woman's answer contained the phrase "that side of the world."

Piatt Street, 1965

Hell that winter
fell in black and white
singed our Sylvanias
smudged our special editions
white jet fuel tongues licked
black smoke streets where
no one we knew ever ventured just a
mile two miles over we felt the boom
tires houses families we'd never
Hey There
cindered
Oh the Negroes Oh my father wept
two months later Bloody Sunday
someone else's families Oh my father said
in black and white turning off the set
the Negroes

At 9:31 AM on Saturday morning, January 16, 1965, a KC-135 Stratotanker crashed into a predominately African-American neighborhood at Piatt & 20th St. in Wichita, Kansas. All seven crew members and 23 people on the ground were killed, with an additional 27 people injured and 15 houses destroyed. On Sunday, March 7, 1965, six hundred Civil Rights marchers crossed the Edmund Pettus Bridge in Selma, Alabama, only to be beaten by State troopers, sheriff's deputies, and posse men. At least 17 marchers were hospitalized and 40 others injured.

Yes the Killers

like a flock of brilliant birds and so
I wrote that poem he says and I say When

was it that you saw them and he says Four years
ago the day after they found that

missing girl's body in the frozen field
over which I saw them floating and I just had this

feeling you know and I say Yes I know I saw them too
just yesterday all yellow and red and blue all

bunched together still like some small hand
had blossomed just a moment ago and set them free

they were headed north it was a sign to me of things to
    come
though the trees were all still bare armed

and so sorrowful there It would be nice
he says if we could all be like balloons Yes I say opening

out my hand it would be nice My name is Blue I add
My name is Red he says I search the sky

on the way back home but all around me is that
field there is no moon and the bone chill night is
    murderous black

like it must have been four years ago and yet somewhere
on the other side of the world it's greening

spring and someone's found little girl lets go a
flock of many colors into the bright beamed face of God

runs laughing open armed towards laughing opening arms
   and so
I write this poem *Madonna And Child, Laughing* for

Red and me the missing nameless all of us yes the
killers too because I just have this feeling you know
   if you ever see

balloons

Up

Fingers pointing, *look there, honey!* an older couple,
moored to the pavement, shopping bags jettisoned like
 ballast,
eyes raised towards a hot air balloon, yellow green
 suspended
in an otherwise flawless ultramarine
that could be

the headscarf of Vermeer's pearl earringed girl, except
it's purer than that, as pure as the dewy radiance of
the girl herself as she dares to stare right back at us,
lips parted, their ruby red pubescence
as enigmatic as

our mysterious celestial navigator's Lilliputian gondola,
itself an earring depending from a bigger earring
 depending
from a canvas only God could paint,
or Jules Verne,
but this is

no five weeks' wonder, no flight of fancy
into deepest darkest Africa, this is an Our Town kind of
 town
in the middle of Mr. and Mrs. America and All the Ships
 at Sea,
which is what this sky maybe looks like, after all,
the sea,

the Mother, the amniotic primeval, life birthed on a
   flood tide of light,
gill-vestiged, shaky limbed, crawling, climbing, striding
   forth upright,
thumbs, fingers prying, chert-pointed, bronze-tipped,
   steel-bladed,
at the oyster in its palm, daring, scarcely do the lips part,
to ask

why, what, who, when, how
did I get here, and you and your wife and I, the only
   ones in the jam-
packed Walmart parking lot who bother to look, fingers
   pointing, up
—the only ones with pearls in our eyes—
say *look there, honey! the sky, the sky*

Spacemen

In 1992, Eileen Dean departed this life, not once, but twice. This is a telling of the days between.

When you see them outside your window we breathe a sigh of relief. You ask what they are doing out there on the roof in those funny suits, floating around like that. The first words you have spoken since your malfunction. Construction, we say. Maintenance. Though we don't really know. We can't see them. We haven't, like you, been to the other side. If you've ever seen spacemen before, you haven't mentioned them. If we could track these particular spacemen down, look out through your eyes, drift in the ether of your slowly returning mind, we'd shake whatever passes for their hands. Ask them in for lunch, figuring hospital food is the same no matter the planet. We question the doctors about the spacemen. They say it's normal for someone coming back from the dead.

The doctors huddle with us. Speak in whispers. Sketch out variants of your future for when the spacemen return to their home planet, as we are assured they will. The doctors wear long white coats and have appendages dangling from their necks. You ask if they too are spacemen, snuck into your room through the air conditioner vent. We too wonder, sometimes. The doctors want to implant things in your body. Experimental, otherworldly things. Top secret. Forms will have to be signed. Consent given. We are shown diagrams. Schematics. Artist's renderings. We are told these will save you. Redeem you, as if you are an object of desire on a cereal box and all we need is enough box tops. We are told these devices will anchor you in our world, on our planet, for another five years. Ten, if lucky. Without them, you will, again, at any moment and without warning, without any chance of return, fail.

We say yes. Yes, to everything. Yes, and as soon as possible. Yes, and yes and yes. We are selfish. We are weak. We are afraid. We love her, we say. We can't live without her. Repair her. Please. On our knees, we say it.

For a week, for an eternity, we watch with you in shifts, our eyes peeled for signs of departing spaceships. The only way we know when they go is when you no longer mention them. Act as if they had never existed. As if they have wiped all trace of themselves from your brain. We act as if, too. We are happy to see them go. Or would have been, had we. Maybe even waved, bye-bye. Thank you for not taking our mother, our wife, to see your leader. Go in peace.

You review the schematics. You are impressed. You are hopeful. Your mind is sharp. Clearer than in years. You embrace the devices. Sign your life away. The doctors high-five. Or would, we suspect, if we weren't here. We suspect. Have begun to suspect. We count our box tops and come up short. The doctors pull box tops from their pockets. They look foreign. Cryptic. Alien. We suspect. We plot. In the middle of the night we will smuggle you out. Hide you in the basement. The garage. For as long as you last. As short as. We are selfish. We are weak. We are afraid. We love you, we say. We can't live without you. The forms. Rip them up. Burn them. On our knees, we ask it.

You take us in your arms. Rock us. Suckle us. Sing to us. Lullabies of time and space. In your eyes, we see ourselves, tiny, naked, reaching. There now, you say. There.

When the doctors come down from surgery they flash thumbs up. She will sleep a while, they say. Go. Sup. Break bread.

In the restaurant, phones ring. Come back. Malfunction. Failure. Oh, come back, quick. The waitress floats towards us with the check. We bundle on our funny suits, slip into hyperspace. Hearts implode. From our eyes, stars fall.

Cleanup on Aisle Five

A glint of copper from the floor separating
Hungry Man from Marie Callender. My father
trying to communicate with me again. I say

again like it happens all the time and not just when I'm
least expecting it, the last time being some twenty-three years
ago, 2 AM, driving home in a tux from a gig and the night
all dressed in mourning, crying, even, raining the tears
I have yet to shed in the six months since he died, and

there he is, aural ectoplasm extruding from my car radio,
manifesting himself in the saccharine alto sax voice
of a John Tesh tune I hate. Devil's advocate is what

he called it, and he played the part whenever he could.
Vietnam, Watergate, Reaganomics, the earth is flat,
you only think you love Jenny, Pamela, Susan. But
that is not why I pulled over under a bridge that night until
my sobbing and the song and the rain and the whole damn
    séance

ended. Not why I pass up the penny and move on
to the aisle of plastic utensils and paper plates
for the lonely eater. No, I am concerned with
appearances, moth-eaten as they may be in my case.

What would people think? A sixty-something man,
stooping to pick up one cent as if it might make the
difference in the rent this month, or the car payment, as if
it were treasure enough to take himself out to a restaurant

and sit across the table from all the empty rooms of his life,
have a conversation with what or whoever might have
filled them, if only he had done this instead of that, called

heads instead of tails, if only the universe had been
a square dealer. Stooping, as my dad always did
when the glint caught his eye. *Lucky penny,*
he would say, grinning like a kid at Christmas,
and in those two words were more of the

Great Depression than in any history book ever written.
Even now the Devil whispers it in my ear as I reach
for the plastic cups: *Lucky penny,* and since there is no
bridge here under which to pull over until the sobbing stops,
I go back into the aisle of the frozen and retrieve my father's
   voice.
It sings from my pocket on the drive home. It serenades me
   still,

from its place on the shelf next to the John Tesh CD I picked
   up
the day after the night of the bridge, an aria daring me

to write it.
To feel
lucky.

And when I glance up from my computer
and out the window at a thousand silver pennies,
the rich night wrapping this round planet
like the warm blanket of my father's arms,

I do.

They Run Free Like a River of Wild Horses
For Caelan

in the high synapse valleys
where the grass is young and tender
and the larkspur and the bluebonnets do not trample
beneath their hooves
listen
you can feel the distant rumble
up through the soles of your memory shoes
as we turn

into a parking lot in the *bad part of town*
per your father's delicate phrasing
though houses sag in other neighborhoods
and miracles are performed here daily
Via Christi
is what they call it now
from the Latin: *a way, passage, journey*
as we ascend

to the cancer floor
where angels tread in blues and greens
plucking hymns from laptops
you tug at me with your still small hand
whisper
a puzzle about a name tree sketched on scrap paper
that day we went to the library
as we enter

the little white house on D Street with its flowery wallpaper
Elsie and Edna scrunched on the sofa like ninety-year old
    schoolgirls
giggling while they rattle the family skeletons
mom and dad egging them on
tape recorder rolling
listen:
these are your grandparents, laughing, your great-great -
    aunts, telling tales
laying an extra place setting for your great-uncle Fred
in the part of town that never grows old
as we do

Llama, 1957
A haibun on the photograph A Llama in Times Square by Inge Morath, New York, 1957

I've travelled 60 years back to this black and white day on West 44th St., not to see Judy Holliday in "Bells Are Ringing" at the Shubert, or Roz Russell in Auntie Mame just down the street, but to see you, you silly thing, poking your long neck out a taxi's rear window as if you are the main attraction, your long ears stiffly up like antennae, listening, no doubt, for applause, or, maybe, news from the future, the latter of which I have: fins on cars (like that Plymouth behind you) went the way of girdles and telephone switchboards. However, perhaps you are prescient in at least some things traffic as there is no human in your taxi and we are working on that very concept right now. Mame, I'm sure, would approve, but probably not Holliday's answering service lady, who is, perhaps, too fond of girdles and telephone switchboards. And, you silly thing, I suppose I must grudgingly concede that on this one particular black and white day in '57 you are, after all, the headliner, the prima donna, the superstar, applause, applause. Just one favor though, if you don't mind, sweetheart:

Stop staring
with those black onyx eyes as if
I'm the oddity here

A Llama in Times Square, Inge Morath, 1957

Sallee's Sallon

It's probably been right there since before the creation
of blow dryers, cuticle nippers, hydrogen peroxide, but,
for reasons known only by that big Max Factor in the sky,
my eyes have just now been opened, a while-supplies-last
Sodom-and-Gomorrah-days redemption sale, as I, Lot-like,
flee, reluctantly as always, the fleshpots and the pleasure
    palaces
of the city.

Probably been right there on the south side of the highway
every god-damned time, coming and going,
wedged between the rusted hulks of Junior's Discount Autos
and the bare-ass-naked windbreak straining to
break wind over a field of porcelain toilets.

Been right there a thousand yards before
the stop sign at the cross roads where
not even the devil shows at midnight,
this cracker-box shrine to pioneer womanhood
and the rustifi-deification of the English language:
Sallee's Sallon
And Beatification Emporium,
peeling paint like dandruff on one hell of a bad hair day.

Right smack-dab there since darkness moved
upon the face of the waters, every kind of beast
was pronounced good, the dust of the earth took form,
inhaled, strode naked and erect through the garden,
causing Lilith to pull at her tangled mane,
scowl into the mirror,
and plot how to steal the only game in town
back from that upstart rib-bone bitch.

Whereupon Sallee said, *Well hun, let's see now. How 'bout—*
a drop dead pixie, deep side part, caramel highlights, glitter
   nails…

Seconds

Walden, is it you?
—Henry David Thoreau

The alarm blinks 8:38,
the microwave 8:37.
HDTV slipstreams in at 8:34
but it's Droid by a nose at 8:33.
Nightmares gallop in reverse this morning
or I've awakened in the Twilight Zone.

I punch Father Time's virtual numbers,
frayed nerves salved by rotary dial clicks.
A bright-voiced man assures me of a bright-eyed future
with a second mortgage from the First National Bank.
The current time is…

*—We're sorry, that number
is no longer in service*

Quickly now from some dusty shelf
WWV on the short wave dial
the Atomic Clock in Boulder CO
    …tick…tick…tick…
    At the tone
Walter Cronkite looks up from the report just handed him
removes his glasses
on the horizon a mushroom cloud

                          In the hills,
the fishermen reel and cast, reel and cast,
the water as blue-deep as memory.
Mom snaps a Polaroid,
Pop threading hooks with night crawlers.
From his perch on my wrist, gloved hands pointing
to the spaces, not the numbers,
Mickey Mouse winks.

This Last Deep Blue Day

In the borderland
between highway and woods

you spy a doe's white belly,
legs stretched straight in rigor,

a fleet dream run down.
You consider stopping,

standing her up,
watching her bound off

into the fire and gold
of this last deep blue day

before December swaggers in,
red jacketed, guns blazing, knives drawn.

Leaves shudder.

You heed the warning
and pass on by. Ahead of you,

the convergence of sky and road
keeps its distance.

Notes:

Chair Car, Edward Hopper, 1965
https://www.wikiart.org/en/edward-hopper/chair-car-1965

Seventeen cats on the front steps of 82 Maple Street, Edward Gorey, 20th Century
https://goreystore.com/products/edward-gorey-17-cats-of-maple-street-print

Nighthawks, Edward Hopper, 1942
https://www.artic.edu/artworks/111628/nighthawks

A Llama in Times Square, Inge Morath, 1957
http://ingemorath.org/a-llama-in-times-square-1957/

Robert L. Dean, Jr.'s work has appeared in *Flint Hills Review, I-70 Review, The Ekphrastic Review, Illya's Honey, Red River Review, River City Poetry, Heartland! Poetry of Love, Resistance & Solidarity,* and the *Wichita Broadside Project*. He read at the 13th Annual Scissortail Creative Writing Festival in April 2018 at East Central University in Ada, Oklahoma, and the Chikaskia Literary Festival 2018 at Northern Oklahoma College, Tonkawa campus. His haibun placed first at Poetry Rendezvous 2017. He was a finalist in the 2014 Dallas Poets Community chapbook contest and a quarter-finalist in the 2018 Nimrod Pablo Neruda Prize for Poetry contest. He is event coordinator for Epistrophy: An Afternoon of Poetry and Improvised Music held annually in Wichita, Kansas. He has been a professional musician and worked at *The Dallas Morning News*. He is a member of the Kansas Authors Club and lives in a one-hundred-year-old stone building in Augusta, Kansas, along with a universe of several hundred books, CDs, LPs, two electric basses and a couple dozen hats.

This project was made possible, in part, by generous support from the Osage Arts Community.

Osage Arts Community provides temporary time, space and support for the creation of new artistic works in a retreat format, serving creative people of all kinds — visual artists, composers, poets, fiction and nonfiction writers. Located on a 152-acre farm in an isolated rural mountainside setting in Central Missouri and bordered by ¾ of a mile of the Gasconade River, OAC provides residencies to those working alone, as well as welcoming collaborative teams, offering living space and workspace in a country environment to emerging and mid-career artists. For more information, visit us at www.osageac.org

www.ingramcontent.com/pod-product-compliance
Lightning Source LLC
Chambersburg PA
CBHW030132100526
44591CB00009B/627